KU-268-060

The Little
Degas

Catherine de Duve

Go behind the scenes at the Opera

**KATE'ART
EDITIONS**

AT THE TIME

Nadar from Honore Daumier

The world is fascinated by a new invention! The first cameras start to appear. What a revolution! The visionary photographer Nadar took the first aerial photograph of Paris in 1858 from his hot air balloon 80 metres up in the air! The writer Jules Verne was influenced by this intrepid act, inspiring his heroic characters in the novel *Five Weeks in a Balloon*, which he wrote in 1862.

Novel by J. Verne

A new fashion from England seizes Paris. Horse racing courses draw large crowds to the Longchamp race course. How exciting!

The English photographer Eadweard Muybridge (1830-1904) studied the movements of men and animals. He made a photographic study of the movement of a horse, Daisy's Gallop, and showed how a galloping horse, for a split second, does not touch the ground.

His trick? 24 cameras installed all along the racetrack. During the race, the horse severs the wire trigger mechanisms one by one, setting off the cameras and capturing its gallop in a series of photos.

Women never go out without a hat. They go to the milliner who provides them with their pretty bonnets. There are hats for all tastes and budgets! The men also dress in smart suits and elegant top hats that cover their heads. "Madame!" They tip their hats to the pretty lady.

Everything is written by hand! Accounts are recorded in huge books. The letters and labels are handwritten. Do you see them in the waste-paper basket?

Find the image where the image where the horse does not touch the ground. Circle it.

COTTON

Edgar de Gas was born in Paris on the 19th of July 1834. He is the eldest of five children: Edgar, Achille, Thérèse, Marguerite and René. His father, Auguste, is the manager of the French office of the family bank, which was founded in Naples, Italy. His mother, Célestine, has Creole origins and is the daughter of a cotton merchant who made his fortune in New Orleans, America.

Unfortunately, his mother dies when he is only 13 years old. His father, a great lover of art and music, takes young Edgar to the Louvre museum to admire the great masterpieces on display. He presents his son to his friends, art collectors and encourages his artistic talent.

In 1855, Edgar enters the School of Fine Arts in Paris where he paints historical scenes, like *Young Spartans Exercising*, which were inspired by Greek Antiquity.

In Ancient Greece, the education of girls in the city of Sparta was very physical, just like for the boys. This causes the rivalry we can see here.

The young painter signs his paintings "Degas". A name of an artist! Bit by bit he distances himself from his classical training so that he can observe and paint the world around him, modern life!

Years later, Degas stays with his uncle Michel Musson in New Orleans. There, many plantations grow the precious material cotton. Edgar paints his uncle in his office, capturing the thriving cotton trade. Do you see the men checking the quality of the cotton? Degas also paints his two brothers, René reading the newspaper and Achille standing cross legged watching the frenzied activity of the office.

What do we do with cotton? How many figures can you count? Find Michel, René and Achille in this picture.

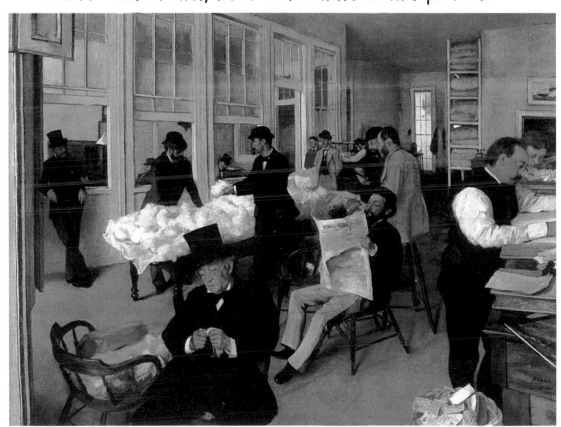

ITALY

Botticelli

Off to Italy! In 1856, the young Degas goes to Italy, discovering Rome, Florence and Naples. He stays there for three years. What beauty! He admires the great masterpieces of the Renaissance, such as the works of Botticelli and Raphaël. He goes to visit his grandfather, René Hilaire de Gas, in Naples, then to Florence to his aunt Laura who is married to the Baron Gennaro Bellelli. The young artist draws numerous pictures of his hosts and their two daughters, Giovanna and Guila, aged 10 and 7 years old.

Raphaël

Who is who? Find the details in the painting

On his return to Paris, Degas paints this ambitious family portrait. Their faces are serious and cold. The motionless objects seem to be hiding a big secret. The atmosphere is dull and tense. Only Giulia, the youngest sister, has a carefree air, her leg resting on the chair. How are the little girls dressed?

What room is the portrait taken in? Explain the relationship between the characters. Are they in a good mood? Who has had his head cut off?

In this picture, we can see the influence of the French painter Ingres (1780-1867) who the young Degas admired and based his early work on. His lines are pure and clear, like those of his old master who he met when he was 21. Ingres gave him the advice: *"Draw lines, young man, and still more lines, both from life and from memory, and you will become a good artist."*

RACE HORSES

The Parisians discover a new passion from England, horse racing! The Emperor Napoleon III builds a race course in the woods of Boulogne at Longchamp that the Parisian bourgeoisie flocks to. It's an opportunity to wear beautiful dresses and stylish outfits, protected from the sun by their top-hats and pretty parasols. The strong sunlight casts the horses' shadows on the ground. Excitement mounts in the stands... Could the race be about to start?

How many jockeys can you count? Find the horse that's out of control!

Degas paints silhouettes of thoroughbreds and of their jockeys wearing their colourful racing outfits.

 It's your turn. Draw a race course.

THE ORCHESTRA

I n the orchestra pit the musicians are focusing upon their musical scores. Degas is allowed to attend their rehearsals thanks to his friend Désiré Dihau, the bassoon player in the Opera's orchestra. Can you see him? His lips are pursed as he blows into his instrument. Can you hear the music? You're in the front row!

Who's playing what? Meet Degas' friends. Place them in his painting. Find the musical instruments. Who's in the royal box?

Dihau on Bassoon

Pillet on Cello

Altes plays the Flute

Gouffé on Contra-bass

Chabrier the Composer

Draw your favourite instrument

On stage, we see only the legs and tutus of the dancers, without heads or feet.
The imprecision of their silhouettes contrasts with the precise detail that Degas
uses for his orchestra.

DANCE CLASS

In the class of the old dancer Jules Perrot, his students are distracted. One is scratching her back, another adjusts her dress, and the third is upset, being comforted by her mother. The old teacher does not seem to notice, instead focusing on the performance of one dancer.

Find the students who are distracted and those paying attention. Have you found the watering can, the piano and the little dog?

After their lessons comes the exam. Dressed all in white the teacher sets the rhythm by beating a long stick. One, two, three! One, two, three! An exercise rail runs along the wall of the room. Whilst they wait, some ballerinas are warming up. In the doorway, one dancer disappears gracefully. Next!

What's the overwhelming colour in this picture? Find the little touches of red and the mirror that bring the painting to life.

COMPOSITION

The master of the ballet is standing at the back of the room observing his dancers. Who's coming down the stairs? The spiral staircase gives a dynamic movement to the composition. It conceals a part of the room, as if Degas is hiding behind it as he watches the ballerinas. A seamstress, busy repairing the tutu of a young girl, takes up the other half of the painting.

Where would the painter be as he paints this scene?

Why does the painter crop his figures?
During the Universal Exhibition in Paris,
Degas visits the Oriental pavilions.
The East is in! He discovers and acquires
a large number of Japanese prints. Their
style is very original. Degas is greatly
inspired by them. He composes his paintings
with new angles and points of view, as he
does with the ballet class, which he divides
between the dancers exercising and those relaxing.
It's daring for its time!

What position are the dancers in the tutus making?
It's your turn. Draw a picture in this original style.

BALLET

The big day is approaching! The ballerinas will soon be in the spotlight. But they must still work. Here they are on the stage in full dress rehearsal. The choreography must be perfect! After numerous entrechats, throws, points and pirouettes they are exhausted. While one group rehearses, the second waits its turn. This is an opportunity to stretch and to retie their ballet-shoes and the ribbons they wear around their necks.

Find the man watching the dancers.
Who could he be?

Degas paints his canvas in grisaille, creating a painting in a slightly ochre shade of gray, like in the photographs of the sepia period. Degas exhibits this intimate painting at the first Impressionist exhibition in 1874 which was held in the studio of the eccentric photographer Nadar.

Where would you watch the show from if you attended the ballet? Would you sit in the stalls, in a box, on the balcony or way up in the gallery?

Shhh...! The ballet's beginning.

Degas chose a new elongated format.
Here he paints the main subject off-centre, as do the Japanese prints he admires. This gives the impression of movement.

THE LITTLE DANCER

Degas is also a sculptor. He creates this dancer out of wax. He first exhibits it at the 1881 Impressionist exhibition in a glass case. Oh! How dreadful! thinks the public who feel a strange, eerie sensation when they see it. Degas' Little Dancer has real hair, and is dressed in slippers and a tutu. The effect is hyper-realist! The critics go wild for it.

After the death of the artist it is made into a bronze sculpture. Here it is dressed in a tutu and with a pink ribbon in her hair. Is she in the middle of her dance routine?

Look at the dancer. How old do you think she is? What material is her costume made out of? What position is she in? Can you make the same pose as her?

Degas was fascinated by movement. Photography allowed him to study the intimate and precise aspects of the body. To study sequences of gestures he creates a series of little wax sculptures throughout his career. 150 small sculptures like this were found in his studio. Here's one in bronze.

The dancer starts to move! Copy her position and imagine your future life as a dancer. Careful! Stay balanced!

Look at these different photographs. Choose one and draw a figure from it.

THE GREEN FAIRY

We're in the café "La Nouvelle Athenes" at the Place Pigalle in Paris, where all the artists come to meet. Here they discuss painting, literature, politics... It's Bohemia. Yet tonight the café seems to be empty. Only two customers are seated, slumped over their drinks. Do they seem rich or poor? The woman fixes the ground with a blank stare. Her face looks deflated and disappointed. Next to her, a man smokes a pipe. What are they saying?

Degas paints this image in his studio. He asked the comedian Ellen André and the engraver Marcellin Desboutin to come and pose for him. However, to avoid a scandal, the painter has to state afterwards that the two models are not actually real alcoholics! He has to protect their reputation!

What colour dominates this picture?
What is the woman drinking? Colour in her drink.

The painting *In the Cafe* is more well-known by the title *Absinthe*, the name of a very popular alcoholic spirit. This alcohol is nicknamed the Green Fairy because of the fennel and mint that gives it its green colour. However, it caused so much drunken chaos in the population that the French government had to ban it! The French writer Emile Zola denounced this drunken scourge of Paris in his novel *L'Assommoir*. *"I simply described, in more than one place in my book, some of your paintings"* he admitted to Degas.

Look at the signs. Which ones are against alcohol?

THE CANNON WOMAN

A ll the artists of Montmartre go to the Circus Fernando. Degas went there four times once! Perhaps it was only to admire the beautiful acrobat Miss La La? Her performance is amazing! Holding a rope with only her clamped teeth, the young trapeze artist is hoisted to the top of the circus tent. At the other end of the rope is attached a cannon. When the acrobat passes just above the audience... BOOM!
The cannon is fired. This is the spectacular, death-defying act of Miss La La, *the cannon woman!*

To create his painting Degas makes many preparatory drawings. The acrobat is suspended by only a wire. "Oh!" the public is afraid for her safety in this dangerous act. All hold their breath out of fear that she might fall... Gasp! What suspense!

What impression does the painting leave you with? Degas uses diagonal lines. Trace these with your finger. What effect do they have on the painting?

Other painters were also inspired by this famous circus. Who are they?

Look at the different types of painting. Which one is "pointillist"?

Seurat, 1891

Renoir, 1879

THE LAUNDRESSES

In the laundrette, the sheets and clothes are washed and ironed on a coal stove. Two women are hard at work. How are they dressed? What colour are their clothes? One of them yawns and holds a bottle in her hand, perhaps filled with water to soften the fabric. The second, arms outstretched, applies pressure to the white sheets with a hot iron. Careful not to burn it! Behind them washed sheets are hung up to dry.

Find the stove, the bed sheets, the iron and the linen in the painting.

The subject of ironing is very rare in painting!
However, Degas paints it from 1869 to 1895.
He paints reality as he sees it. He does not hide
the misery. Picasso would later be inspired by Degas' work.
Degas paints the picture directly on to canvas, without a preparatory
layer. The oil and pastel colours are rough on the fabric.

In his book *L'Assommoir*, Zola was inspired by Degas' focus on the
theme of ironing. His heroine, Gervaise, hires two women to iron in
her laundrette. According to the writer, *"it's the first novel about people
who do not lie and who have the actual smell of real people."*
Zola is the spokesman for the misery of the Parisian people
and becomes famous.

Colour the laundresses in with pastel colours of
your choice. What soft colours!

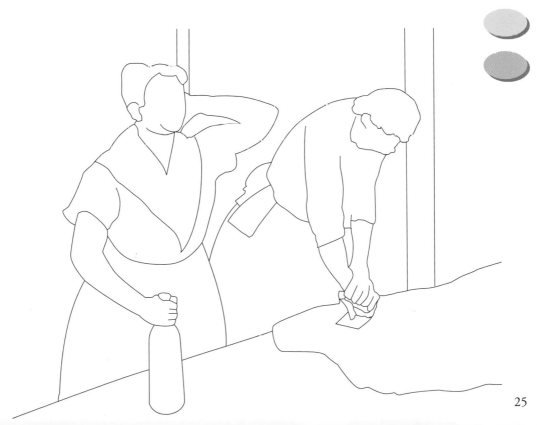

BATHING

At the time of Degas, not everyone has a well equipped bathroom. Running water does not exist yet! To wash, people have to use a jug of water and a sponge in a large basin called a tub, or for the better off, a deep bath.

The painter produces a series of paintings devoted to women washing themselves. Degas captures their intimate moments.

A Natural Sponge

A woman crouched in the basin presses a sponge to her neck. What are the items on the dresser?

Find the hairbrush, the jug, the red hairpiece and her curling tongs. Where is the light coming from? What colour are the shadows?

"I am a colourist with the line" Degas confirms. In the late 19th century Degas reintroduces the pastel technique to his work. Due to its texture it helps create the effect of fabric and skin, emphasising the effect of light on objects.

Pastel is a technique in drawing. It uses small sticks made up of chalk, plaster and colour pigments which are bound with Arabic gum for dry pastels, or with oil and later with wax for oil pastels.

Pastels

Look at the pastel effect. Objects come to life thanks to the different pastel colours being applied in fine strokes.

In the milliner's workshop feathers and flowers form pretty spots of colour on the work table. A woman wearing a white apron holds a blue feather out for the hat maker. Who is she? The making of a hat requires many beautiful accessories. Who is the beautiful hat being made for and for what occasion? To show off at the horse races, to go to the opera, to the Salons, or to walk in the Tuileries Gardens and listen to a concert?

Now it's your turn. Decorate your hat with feathers and flowers.

STROLLING

These paintings are the memories of Degas' strolls through the streets of Paris. The cafés, the studios and behind the scenes...

🔍 **Where would you like to go with the painter?**

To the hat maker   *To the laundrette*   *To the dance rehearsals*

To the Horse race   *To the Circus*   *To Manet's house*

Backstage at the opera   *To the ballet*   *To the café*

Degas never marries but has many friends. Every Thursday he visits Edouard Manet, at whose house he meets the poet Stéphane Mallarmé and the painter Pierre-Auguste Renoir.

Unfortunately the painter gradually loses his sight. During the last decade of his life he becomes almost blind. Soon he has to abandon all artistic creation. However, that does not stop him from strolling along the boulevards of Paris into his old age.

Edgar Degas died on the 27th September 1917 aged 83. He is buried in the cemetery of Montmartre in Paris. He asked that only sentence be inscribed on his gravestone:

"He loved drawing".

Text: Catherine de Duve
Concept and Production: Kate'Art Editions
Research: Frédérique Masquelier
Proof-reading: Carole Daprey
Translation from the French: Stuart Forward

Photographic credits:
Edgar Degas: **Paris:** Musée d'Orsay: *Blue Dancers*, c.1893: cover, p. 1, p. 30 – *The Parade also known as Race Horses* 1866-1868: cover, p. 2, pp.8-9, p. 30 – *The Bellelli Family*, c.1858-1860: p. 6, p. 7 – *Horse with Jockey*; *Horse Galloping on Right Foot*, 1865-1890: p. 8 – *The Orchestra at the Opera House*, c.1868-1869: p. 10, p. 11 – *The Dance Class*, c. 1873-76: p. 12, p. 30- *Ballet Rehearsal on the Set*, 1872: cover, p. 13 – *Ballet Rehearsal on Stage*, 1874: p. 16 – *Little Fourteen-Year-Old Dancer*, 1879-1881: p. 18 – *Dancer Fourth Position Front, on Left Leg*, 1896-1911: p. 19 – *Spanish Dance, Second Study*, 1882-1885: p. 19 – *In the café or The Absinthe Drinker*, c.1875-1876: p. 20, p. 30 – *Laundresses*, c.1884-1886: p. 24, p. 30 – *The Tub*, 1886: p. 26 – *Woman in her Bath, Sponging her Leg*, 1883: p. 26- *After the Bath, Woman Drying her Left Foot*, 1886: p. 27 – *At the Milliner's*, c.1898: p. 28, p. 30 – *Harlequin and Colombine*, c.1886-1890: p. 30 | **Pau:** Musée des Beaux-Arts: *Portraits in a New Orleans Cotton Office*, 1873: p. 3, p. 5 | **London:** The Samuel Courtauld Trust, The Courtauld Gallery: *Two dancers on a stage*, c.1874: cover, p. 17 – The National Gallery: *Spartan Girls Challenging Boys (Young Spartans Exercising)*, c.1860: p. 4 – *Miss La La at the Circus Fernando*, 1879: p. 23, p. 30 | **Glasgow:** Burrell Collection: *The Rehearsal*, c.1874: p. 14, p. 15 – *Grande Arabesque, first time*, 1882-1890: p. 19 ©Culture and Sport Glasgow (Museums) | **New-York:** The Metropolitan Museum of Art: *At the Milliner's*, 1882: cover, p. 3 | **Boston:** Museum of Fine-Arts: *Racehorses at Longchamp*, 1871-1874: p. 9 | **Kitakyushu (Japan):** *Portrait of Monsieur and Madame Édouard Manet*, c.1868-1869: p. 30 | Others: Eadweard Muybridge: **London:** Royal Academy of Arts: *Daisy's Gallop*, 1872-1885: p. 3 – *Dancing (fancy)*, 1872-1885: p. 19 | Archives: Honoré Daumier: *Nadar in a balloon*, 1869: p. 2 – *Illustration for "Five Weeks in a Balloon" by Jules Verne*: p. 2 – Poster F. Monod, *L'Absinthe c'est la mort*, 1905: p. 21 – Christol: *L'Alcool! Voila l'ennemi*, 1910: p. 21 - Tamagno: *L'absinthe Oxygénée*, 1896: p. 21 | **Florence:** The Offices: Botticelli: *The Birth of Venus*, c.1485: p. 6 – Raphaël: *Madonna and Child*, 1504-1505: p. 6 | Seurat: **Paris:** Musée d'Orsay: *The Circus*, 1891: p. 22 | Renoir: **Chicago:** Art Institute of Chicago: *The Circus Fernando*, 1879: p. 22

Thanks to: Ann Dumas, curator Royal Academy, Darran McLaughlin, Royal Academy, Frédérique Masquelier, Olivier Olbrechts, Stuart Forward, Véronique Lux, Carole Daprey and all those who contributed to the creation of this book.

The works of Kate'Art Editions are available in a variety of languages: French, English, Dutch, Spanish, German, Russian, Japanese and Danish.

Visit our online shop: **www.kateart.com**